I0477440

13 More LAWS Of

DEXTER THE EDUCATOR

Principles For Purpose and Success

DEXTER J. HUMPHREY
B.S.E.E., M.A.L.S., M.A.C.E.

13 More Laws
of Dexter The Educator

by
Dexter J. Humphrey
aka Dexter The Educator

Jasa Leadership Group

www.DexterHumphrey.com

www.JasaLeadership.com

Jasa Leadership Group is an educational resource firm that develops products, strategies, and initiatives for students, parents, and academic leaders. Our educational mission: Every student reading and Every student learning.

This Book Belongs To The Person Committed To Improving Themselves:

_____

Full Name

Continue Reading If You Want To Win!

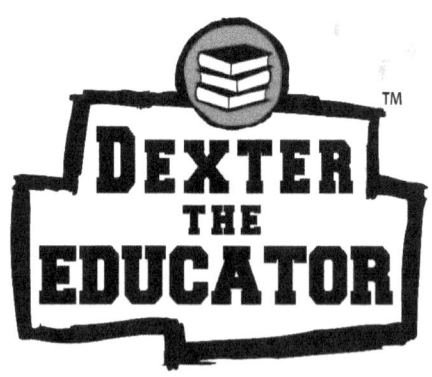

Table of Contents

www.DexterHumphrey.com

Introduction:

<u>Keys To Living Your Dreams</u>

Where is the wealthiest place on the planet? Is it in the halls of the Federal Reserve? Or in the gold vaults of Fort Knox? Or perhaps the oil fields in the Middle East? I submit that the wealthiest place on earth is the graveyard for here rests millions of individuals who died never realizing their potential of depositing their gifts, talents and dreams in the world before they transitioned. The earth is full of people with brilliant ideas, strategies or ingenious possibilities for enhancing the world. However, like many residing in the cemetery, these ideas are hidden and buried within the mind and heart locked away from the world to enjoy.

Success is not an accident. It is the result of a well-executed plan. Keys to living your dreams and achieving success require several fundamental and essential components. The first step in living your dreams requires an acknowledgement of your gifts, talents and skills. All business operates within a medium of exchange in the areas of providing a product or service. So the question is: What can you do that someone will be willing to pay for? Next, you must be willing to invest in your craft. Every great and gifted individual invests countless hours and resources developing themselves through educational training and self-improvement. If your library is barren, then your fruits of

1

achievement will never manifest. To be is to study, what you study you will become!

Finally, in order to live your dreams, you must network with others. If you do not NETWORK, you may NOT WORK. An idea that is not communicated does not exist. Make it your priority to connect with other individuals who are doing what you want to do and with others who are smarter than you. If you are always the smartest person in your circle of associates, then you need to upgrade your environment. Remember, success will never manifest itself, if you leave your gifts, talents and skills sitting on the shelf! Do yourself a favor and prepare for success.

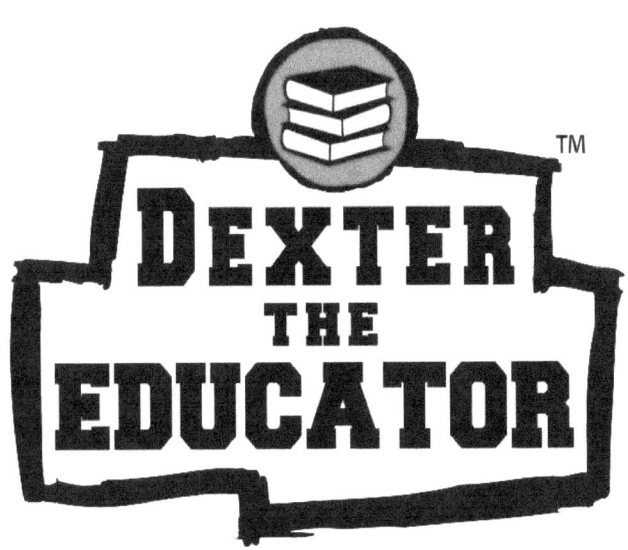

DREAMS
WITHOUT
A PLAN
BECOME
NIGHTMARES.

www.DexterHumphrey.com

What IF...

What If...
You Hustled more than you Dreamed?
What If...
You LOVED more than you Hated?
What If...
You Healed more than you Harmed?
What If...
You Believed more than you Doubted?
What If...
You kept the Faith rather than lived in Fear?
What If...
You Encouraged more than you Criticized?
What If...
You Gave more than you Received?
What If...
You Saved more than you Spent or Shopped?
What If...
You Worked more than you Slept?
What If...
You Read more that you watched TV?
What If...
You owned a Business rather than Worked
for someone else?
What If...
You Prayed more than you Complained?
What would your life or world be like
If the BEST of you aimed at maximizing
the BEST in Others?

4

The Law of Faith

Without Faith, Success Is Impossible.

Faith is a firm conviction or persuasion evidenced by corresponding action. The Law of Faith is absolutely essential as it relates to achieving and succeeding. Faith represents that sustaining quality which brings what you desire into abundance in your life.

Faith says keep going when progress seems impossible. Faith compels your heart to trust in your purpose, path and plans amidst the pains of adversity. Faith guarantees victory against overwhelming odds. It is your faith in what you are destined to do that makes the difference.

Feed your faith and starve your doubts. Doubt arises from the fear of failure. Fear, in all actuality, is the direct opposite and enemy of faith. If faith brings what you desire, then fear brings what you do not desire. Countless individuals have forfeited the fulfillment of accomplishing their dreams because of fear. Do not allow fear to add your name to its list of casualties. Do not allow fear to paralyze you.

When challenges arise, access your persevering spirit of faith and remember why you started working towards your dream(s) in the first place. Use your fears as a motivator to unlock the power of your faith to achieve success. The Law of Faith affirms that all things are possible to those that believe. Fight the good fight of faith as you work towards fulfilling your purpose. Keep the faith…Keep Believing…Trust in your Greatness!

Faith Activity

1. List 3 things you desire in life. _____

_____

_____

2. Describe the steps you are taking to accomplish your goals.

_____

_____

3. List your greatest fear(s). _____

_____

_____

4. (T /F) Acknowledging your fears is the first step to overcoming them.

5. Fill in the blanks.
_____ your faith and _____ your doubts.

6. What is the archenemy of faith?

_____

7. Define Faith. _____

_____

_____

6

KEEP THE FAITH.

KEEP BELIEVING.

TRUST IN YOUR GREATNESS.

www.DexterHumphrey.com

Notes

The Law of The Coach

Proverbs 15:22 Without counsel plans fail; but with many advisers they succeed.

Seldom, if ever, does success come without the aid of coaches, counselors, trainers or advisers. Success is not achieved in a vacuum. Like a perfectly baked cake, success requires many contributing ingredients to yield the desired results. The contributions of others, whether directly or indirectly, play a vital role in the accomplishment of any endeavor. Successful people are coached or developed by other successful people. Success always leaves clues.

Woe unto the person who fails to secure the knowledge, wisdom and experience of coaches and advisers. No matter what you are seeking to achieve, someone exists possessing some expertise or valuable insight to contribute to your aspirations. Great coaching is available from people, books, seminars, classes, webinars, podcasts, conferences or the like. "Not having is no excuse for not getting," the saying goes.

A great coach will bring out the best in you. Great coaching accepts you the way you are but refuses to leave you that way. A great coach will celebrate your strengthens and improve on your weaknesses. The Law of Coaching thrives on developing, empowering and correcting. Submitting yourself to another via coaching is an investment guaranteed to produce bountiful dividends for years to come. Are you coachable?

9

Coaching Activity

Every successful person, regardless of their field, owes a great deal of their success to great coaching or advisers. Find the name(s) of the coach for the individuals listed below.

1. Oprah Winfrey _____
2. Floyd Mayweather _____
3. Les Brown _____
4. Bill Gates _____
5. Tom Brady _____
6. Michael Jordan _____
7. Neil deGrasse Tyson _____
8. Mae C. Jemison _____
9. Martin Luther King Jr. _____
10. Baraka Obama _____
11. T.D. Jakes _____
12. Jeff Gordon _____
13. Mike Kryzweski _____
14. Jeff Bezos_____
15. Suze Orman _____
16. Dennis Kimbo _____

It's Your TEAM Not Your TALENT That Produces Success.

www.DexterHumphrey.com

<u>Notes</u>

The Law of Silence

Isaiah 30:15 In quietness and in confidence
shall be your strength.
Ecclesiastes 3:7 A Time To Keep Silent;

Don't talk about it…Be about it! Many people fail to accomplish their goals and dreams simply because they talk too much. Denzel Washington said in the movie *American Gangster*, "The loudest one in the room is the weakest one in the room." Successful people do not broadcast their next moves to everyone. Goal-Getters think, prepare, plan and execute without seeking the attention of those that do not matter. Everyone does not need to know all of your plans, ideas, or course of action. An African Proverb says, "A fool utters his whole heart." Learn to keep your mouth closed and your mind and hands working.

A fundamental law in the art of war requires concealing your position from the enemy. The Law of Silence mandates secrecy and internal focus. Only share your goals or objectives on a need-to-know basis. Wisdom advocates sharing your plans only with those capable and qualified to assist you in achieving success. Do not error in feeding your critics or haters with privileged information that does not concern them. Talk is cheap but action brings satisfaction.

The Law of Silence Activity

1. Name the first person you would contact with a new idea or potential business move.

    _____

2. What is your first inclination when confronted with a problem or crisis?

    A. Talk to a close relative   C. Pray or Meditate

    B. Deal it to yourself   D. Seek counsel from
                                             a trusted source

3. Which television character do you identify with the most?

    A. Olivia Pope   C. Sydney Bristow

    B. House M.D.   D. Luscious Lyon

4. When and with whom is the best time to share privileged information?

    _____

    _____

5. Describe an incident when speaking about a matter rather remaining silent caused problem(s) for you. _____

    _____

    _____

    _____

    _____

    _____

    _____

    _____

Hustle In Silence;
Let Success
Make The
Noise.

www.DexterHumphrey.com

Notes

The Law of Focus

*"Obstacles Are What We See
When We Take Our Focus Off Our Goals."*

Dr. Myles Monroe stated, "If you don't know where you are going, any road will take you there." Without purpose, direction and focus, failure is inevitable. Those who know what they want and believe in themselves remain focused regardless of the circumstances. The enemy of vision is sight. Do not become victim of losing focus due to perceived obstacles, adversities and resistance. True success only arrives after you have endured and persevered through incessant challenges.

A byproduct of focus is tunnel vision. Once you zero in on your target, nothing else should warrant your time or energy. When you are locked in on your goals, everything else should not garner your attention. The bull's eye always resides in the center, not on the periphery. Focus produces greatness. Focus rewards dedication with success. Focus requires unity of purpose, effort, energy and resilience. Stay focused…do the work…accomplish your dreams. The Law of Focus requires filling your agenda with what's necessary and beneficial.

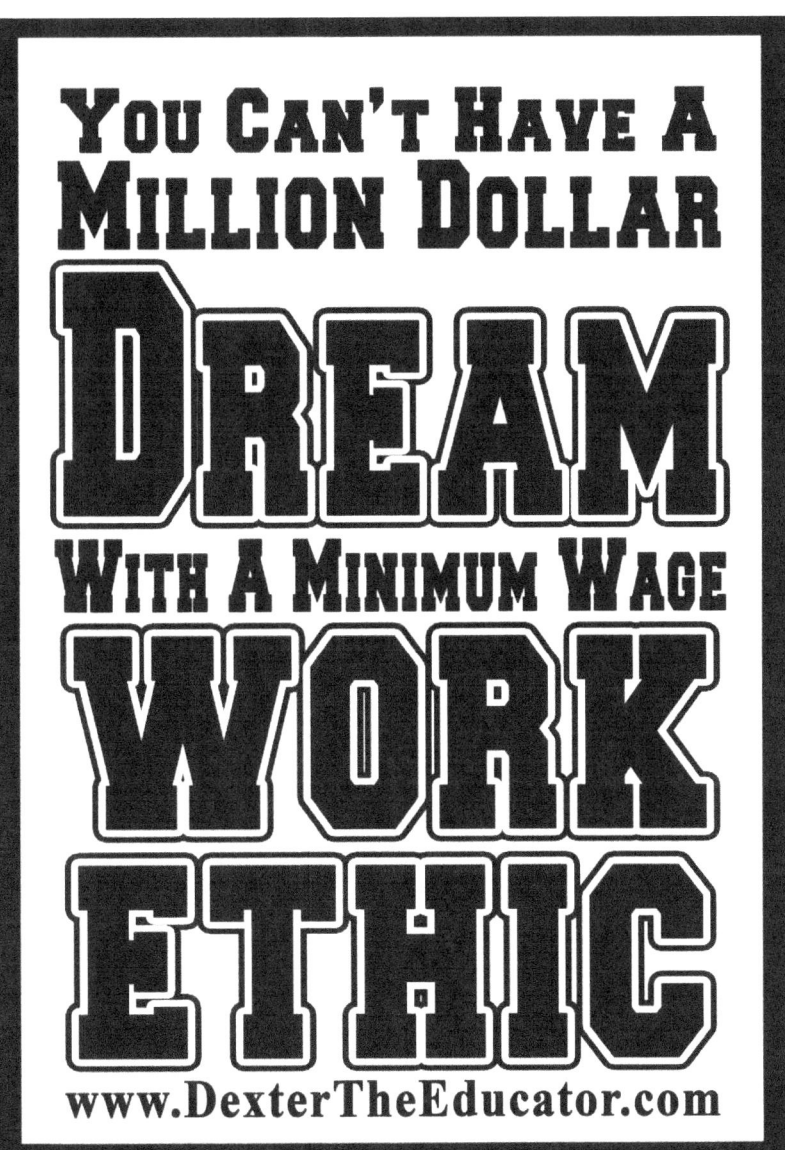

www.DexterTheEducator.com

Focus Activity

1. It takes 30 days to form a habit. Identify one skill you will commit to developing over the next 30 days.

   _____

2. Name 3 great business leaders who achieved excellence by implementing focus and dedication to their craft. _____

   _____

   _____

3. Identify one of your bad habits. Next, establish a 3 to 5 step plan you will execute to eliminate this particular bad habit. _____

   _____

   _____

   _____

4. True or False: The only place where success comes before work is in the dictionary.

5. Fill in the blanks: The enemy of _____ is

   _____.

Notes

The Law of Adjustments

"The Road To Success Does Not Occur In A Straight Line." –Steve Harvey

As brilliant as you are or as remarkable your plans may be, things will NOT go exactly as you desire. The key to survival in any endeavor rests in your ability to adjust, adapt and improvise. Many teams have won championships after horrible starts by making necessary adjustments during the course of a game (e.g. 2017 Super Bowl: New England Patriots vs. Atlanta Falcons).

People who are set in their ways and refuse to adjust will never succeed or realize their full potential. Problems and challenges are par for the course when chasing your dream(s). Murphy's Law will inevitably rear its frustrating head as you pursue that which is important. If what you are doing is not yielding the desire results, make adjustments! Don't succumb to the ills of your pride by insisting things go a specific way. Analyze the situation, seek wise counsel, make the necessary adjustments and relaunch.

Failures are only temporary signposts of the adjustments that need to be made. When things do not add up as planned, start subtracting by implementing corrective actions. Success is on the other side of your adjustments. The true definition of insanity is doing the same thing and expecting different results.

Making adjustments is not an admission of failure but rather a splendid display of wisdom. The objective of your mission seeks victory, not the frustrations of failure. It is in your best interest to do whatever is necessary to insure that you win. If it requires a change in your personal or business relationships, make the adjustments. If it requires a change in your daily routine or schedule, make the adjustments. If it requires reconstructing, rebranding and relaunching, make the adjustments. The Law of Adjustment is a tool for your benefit…use it!

If You Don't Make Adjustments, Your Competition Will.

www.DexterHumphrey.com

23

Notes

The Law of Passion

"Passion not potential produces powerful production!"

Passion represents an intense desire, yearning or an insatiable will to perform or act. Passion compels one to transform from what you could do to what you are fervently doing. Average people go through the motions of life but passionate people dominate every aspect of their lives. Passion paralyzes fear and overcomes the criticism of others through positive and productive actions. Passion propels you to persist in the midst of pain, adversity or overwhelming odds. In essence, passion asks, "How bad do you want it?"

Possessing the ability to channel your passion into fulfilling your purpose embodies the ultimate goal of living. Passion harnesses its kinsman of self-discipline enabling you to perfect your craft. Passion without action is an oxymoron. Passion promotes action, results and the immediate impact of your presence. Successful individuals operate with a level of passion that separates them from the crowd. Passion forces us all to work for what we want, for as long as it takes and investing whatever it takes. The passionate ones do what they are supposed to do, when they are supposed to do it even if they do not feel like it. Passion produces results for reasons beyond a paycheck or the acknowledgment of others. Passion is the driving force for greatness.

SUCCESS

IS NOT AN ACCIDENT; IT IS THE RESULT OF A WELL EXECUTED PLAN.

www.DexterTheEducator.com

Notes

The Law of Haters
Haters Are Gonna Hate!

While haters are hating…just keep winning. Malcolm X proffered an axiom of truth when he posited that if you have no critics then you are not making an impact. Haters only throw "shade" on those winners and game changers who are shining brightly within their purpose. "If you get drunk off of people's compliments, you will die off of their criticisms," T.D. Jakes. The main supporter, encourager and motivator in your life must be you.

If you quit in the face of criticism from haters, then you did not truly want to be successful. Les Brown stated it best by professing, "People's opinion of you does not have to become your reality." Although your haters or detractors have the right to talk negatively about you, you have just as much right NOT to listen. When haters start hating, it's time for you to start vacating. Refuse to allow yourself to become a garbage disposal for the negativity of others. Life is about becoming the best you that you can be. Anyone not subscribing to your vision, goals and dreams should be immediately cut, traded, fired, replaced and removed from your life! TRUTH: NO HATER HATIN' AGAINST ME SHALL PROSPER.

WHILE THEY KEEP HATIN', YOU KEEP WINNING!

www.DexterHumphrey.com

<u>Notes</u>

The Law of The Follow-Up
Learn To Follow Up Or Else!

The key to any endeavor involves establishing strong and meaningful relationships. An axiom of business representing one of my core beliefs affirms, "If you do not NETWORK, you will NOT WORK." However, many individuals who initially invest the time effort and energy into networking fail to nurture these new introductions by following up.

Any experienced salesperson understands that most sales do not occur on the initial introduction or pitch. Only after carefully and purposefully building a relationship with a prospective client is a sale or deal consummated. The reason why corporations and advertisers utilize celebrities to endorse their product or service is because they understand the power of relationships. It is not so much the product or service that guarantees a sale or deal but rather the relational bond created between the consumer and the supporting influential branding agents or celebrities.

There is no set formula or methodology for following up with those whom you desire to interact with in business. One principle of business directly correlates to your level of success and that is: *Where there is no follow-up, there will be no deal.* Individuals conduct business with people they know and trust.

31

Failing to follow-up to build a relationship with others shows an indifference to their needs.

A brand simply represents the relational reputation established by a company. Relationships always trump any product or service. You can have a world-class, state-of-the-art product or service but if you fail to establish a meaningful relationship with prospective clients, you will soon be out of business. The Law of the Follow-Up involves building relationships.

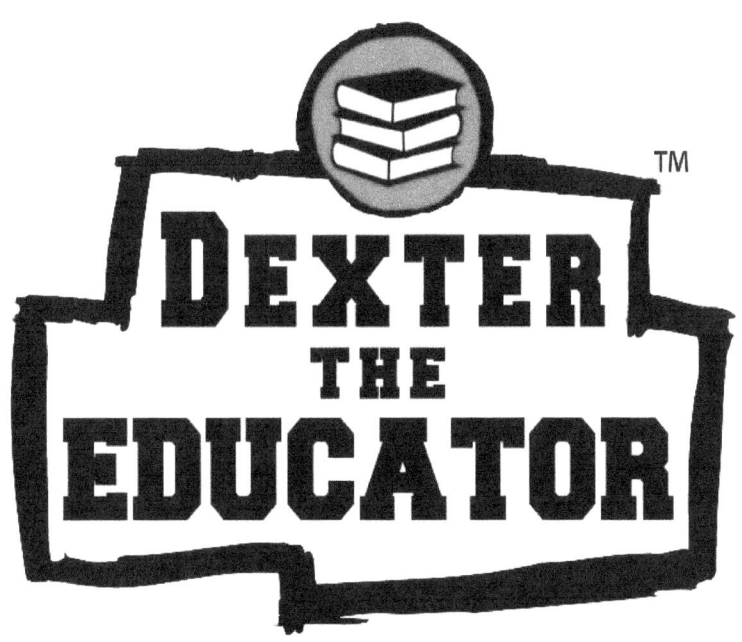

Learn

To

FOLLOW-UP

Or

You Plan

To Fail.

www.DexterHumphrey.com

Notes

<u>The Law of Perseverance</u>
Do Yourself A Favor…Accomplish Your Goals!

Anything worth achieving inevitably brings adversity, setbacks and pain. In order to accomplish your goals, you must handle and overcome the pressure to quit. If you want it, be fortuitous enough to fight for it. The glory of success is worth the arduous journey required to achieve it. If fulfilling your dreams were easy, everyone would become successful.

Before life rewards you with privilege, success or promotion, you will be tested with suffering, failure and adversity. When the moment of truth arrives begging you to quit, give up and cave in; keep going, keep fighting, keep working and keep winning. It's in you to be great. It's in you to succeed and accomplish your dreams. Do not cheat yourself out of the success that is rightfully yours by quitting.

Failure never wins if you don't quit. Allow pain and adversity to serve as your vitamins for greatness. Believe in yourself and trust in the work you put in to place you in the maximized position to win. Believe in your abilities and your competitive spirit. Success and fulfillment reside on the other side of your perseverance. In order to keep winning, you must keep going! Do yourself a favor and DON'T QUIT!

You Could Quit, Give Up And Cave In... But Why?

www.DexterHumphrey.com

36

Notes

The Law of Purpose
Without Purpose, Plans Fail.

Purpose represents your WHY. Purpose speaks to your original intent or motive(s). When purpose is intact, the foundation for success rests on solid ground. Devoid of fully understanding your purpose, it is impossible to maintain focus, passion and perseverance. Knowing why you're embarking on your path provides a vital component for achieving greatness and significance.

One of the worst motives for doing anything is for the love of money. If money drives your ideas or efforts, then discontentment, disappointment and ultimately failure will become your intimate companions. It is perfectly fine to earn money while you are making a difference. Working for free does not represent a sustainable formula for living. However, allow your WHY, not financial gain, to propel your actions.

Purpose aids in maintaining focus and dedication. Direction remains clear when purpose is known. When you know what are called to do and why you are functioning in your given capacity, then resisting distractions becomes second nature. Many individuals lose their way when they lose their WHY. Use your gifts, talents and skills to change the world. Do what you do for the right reasons and fulfillment will always reward your efforts.

Purpose Activity

1. Who are you? _____

   _____

2. What can you do? _____

   _____

3. Write your personal vision statement in one sentence.

   _____

   _____

   _____

4. Write your personal or business mission statement.

   _____

   _____

   _____

5. List at least 2 of your strengths. _____

   _____

6. List at least 2 of your weaknesses. _____

   _____

7. What do you think about the most? _____

   _____

8. Name two persons closest to you and list their
   greatest quality. _____

   _____

   _____

PEOPLE
LOSE THEIR
WAY
WHEN THEY
LOSE THEIR
WHY.

www.DexterHumphrey.com

Notes

The Law of Self-Development
The Only Thing Constant In Life Is Change.

Are you a Timex watch type individual living in the Digital Age? Have you taken it upon yourself to improve your skillset and knowledge base? What steps are you implementing to make your good better and your better to become your best? The Law of Self-Development warrants constant upgrades for increased productivity and relevance. How many mobile apps would remain viable in the marketplace if they were not constantly updated to improve performance?

As you strive to fulfill your dreams, be sure to invest in your self-development. It may require enrolling in a class or specialized training; or attending a few seminars or conferences. There is an abundance of free online tutorials or webinars qualified to enhance your goals of self-development. A noted scholar once proffered, "All I know is all I have studied. And all I have studied is not all there is to know." In essence, there is always room for growth, development and self-improvement. Refusing to grow and increase your capabilities is a recipe for failure. You can either get better or prepare to be terminated. As my uncle use to say, "Tighten up (e.g. Get better) every chance you get!"

Self-Development Activity

1. Explain why the following companies failed.

   A. U.S. Steel _____

   _____

   B. Eastman Kodak _____

   _____

   C. Blockbuster Video _____

   _____

2. List three areas for self-improvement.

   _____

   _____

3. List 3 classes, seminars or trainings you will attend within the next 6 months.

   _____

   _____

   _____

4. List two books you will STUDY to develop yourself.

   _____

   _____

   _____

5. Identify one negativity habit you will terminate from your life. _____

   _____

EVERY DAY
IS THE
RIGHT TIME
TO GET
BETTER!

www.DexterHumphrey.com

44

<u>Notes</u>

<u>The Law of Getting Back Up</u>
Winners May Fall Down but WE Get Back Up!

At age 7	His family lost their home due to poverty and he was forced to work to provide family support.
At age 9	His mother died.
At age 10	His father abandon him for almost a year.
At age 22	His business failed.
At age 23	He lost in the State of Illinois Legislature race for the General Assembly. He also lost his job and was rejected from enrolling into Law School.
At age 24	He borrowed money along with his business partner to start a business. Within a year, his business partner died and their business failed. He was forced to spend the next 17 years repaying their business debt by himself.
At age 25	Lost again for the State Legislature.
At age 26	After becoming engaged to the love of his life, his fiancée died.
At age 27	He suffered a nervous breakdown, coupled with severe depression and became bedridden for 6 months.
At age 29	He ran for Speaker of the State Senate and lost.
At age 33	He ran for Elector and lost.
At age 34	He suffered another nervous breakdown.
At age 36	He campaigned for Congress and lost.
At age 41	After winning a seat in Congress, he ran for re-election and lost.
At age 42	He applied for a land officer job and was denied.
At age 47	He ran for a United State Senate seat and lost.
At age 49	Boldly campaigning for the nomination for Vice President, he was rejected by his own party by receiving less than 100 votes.
At age 51	He attempted to run for a United State Senate seat again and lost for a second time.

At age 53   He was elected President of the United States.

One of the Kings of Getting Back Up…
Abraham Lincoln.

EVERYONE FALLS DOWN BUT NOT EVERYONE GETS BACK UP

www.DexterHumphrey.com

<u>Notes</u>

The Law of Patience
With Faith and Patience, you can inherit the promises of success.

Patience denotes the act of waiting upon a desire result. Moving too fast or too soon practically guarantees the untimely destruction of your life's work. Exercising patience is not a license for laziness or unproductivity. The fundamental Law of Patience dictates your active engagement while waiting on things beyond your control or influence to manifest.

The process of patience provides ample time for growth, maturity and development. Partaking of a fruit before it ripens yields an unpleasant experience. Do not be in a hurry for success, prestige or power. Your hour of excellence will arrive if you allow patience to complete its divine work in your life.

How many athletes have thwarted their promising careers by entering the professional ranks too early? How many entrepreneurs have experienced bankruptcy as a result of launching or expanding their business too soon? Success achieved too quickly will not last. The process to greatness can be just as sweet as the joys of achievement. Time invested in preparation and development is not time wasted. You can be successful if you exercise the Law of Patience and learn to wait!

A Fruit Picked Before Its Time, Spoils Dessert.

www.DexterHumphrey.com

Notes

Seeing Yourself

"Everybody Should Have A Dream!"

See Yourself

See Yourself
Accomplishing your dreams
See Yourself
Fulfilling your purpose
See Yourself
Achieving your vision
See Yourself
Overcoming Obstacles
See Yourself
Persevering in spite of temporary failures
See Yourself
Conquering all challenges
See Yourself
Destroying your doubts
See Yourself
Walking in wealth
See Yourself
Inspiring others
See Yourself
Blessing people's lives
See Yourself
Changing people's lives
See Yourself
Leaving a prosperous legacy
See Yourself
Just See Yourself...

Dexter Humphrey
www.DexterHumphrey.com

If You Can't See Success For Youself, No One Else Will.

Notes

Profiles of Successful People

Complete the profiles of 20 individuals you consider successful.
FACT: Success Leaves Clues.

Name _____

Hometown _____

Date of Birth _____

Highest Education Level _____

College / University _____

Business Name _____

Field of Business _____

Website _____

Product or Service Provided _____

_____

Personal Strengthens _____

_____

Personal Weaknesses _____

_____

Coach or Advisor _____

Name _____

Hometown _____

Date of Birth _____

Highest Education Level _____

College / University _____

Business Name _____

Field of Business _____

Website _____

Product or Service Provided _____

_____

Personal Strengthens _____

_____

Personal Weaknesses _____

_____

Coach or Advisor _____

Name _____

Hometown _____

Date of Birth _____

Highest Education Level _____

College / University _____

Business Name _____

Field of Business _____

Website _____

Product or Service Provided _____

_____

Personal Strengthens _____

_____

Personal Weaknesses _____

_____

Coach or Advisor _____

Name _____

Hometown _____

Date of Birth _____

Highest Education Level _____

College / University _____

Business Name _____

Field of Business _____

Website _____

Product or Service Provided _____

_____

Personal Strengthens _____

_____

Personal Weaknesses _____

_____

Coach or Advisor _____

Name _____

Hometown _____

Date of Birth _____

Highest Education Level _____

College / University _____

Business Name _____

Field of Business _____

Website _____

Product or Service Provided _____

_____

Personal Strengthens _____

_____

Personal Weaknesses _____

_____

Coach or Advisor _____

Name _____

Hometown _____

Date of Birth _____

Highest Education Level _____

College / University _____

Business Name _____

Field of Business _____

Website _____

Product or Service Provided _____

_____

Personal Strengthens _____

_____

Personal Weaknesses _____

_____

Coach or Advisor _____

Name _____

Hometown _____

Date of Birth _____

Highest Education Level _____

College / University _____

Business Name _____

Field of Business _____

Website _____

Product or Service Provided _____

_____

Personal Strengthens _____

_____

Personal Weaknesses _____

_____

Coach or Advisor _____

Name _____

Hometown _____   _____

Date of Birth _____

Highest Education Level _____

College / University _____

Business Name _____

Field of Business _____

Website _____

Product or Service Provided _____

_____

Personal Strengthens _____

_____

Personal Weaknesses _____

_____

Coach or Advisor _____

Name _____

Hometown _____

Date of Birth _____

Highest Education Level _____

College / University _____

Business Name _____

Field of Business _____

Website _____

Product or Service Provided _____

_____

Personal Strengthens _____

_____

Personal Weaknesses _____

_____

Coach or Advisor _____

Name _____

Hometown _____

Date of Birth _____

Highest Education Level _____

College / University _____

Business Name _____

Field of Business _____

Website _____

Product or Service Provided _____

_____

Personal Strengthens _____

_____

Personal Weaknesses _____

_____

Coach or Advisor _____

Name _____

Hometown _____

Date of Birth _____

Highest Education Level _____

College / University _____

Business Name _____

Field of Business _____

Website _____

Product or Service Provided _____

_____

Personal Strengthens _____

_____

Personal Weaknesses _____

_____

Coach or Advisor _____

Name _____

Hometown _____

Date of Birth _____

Highest Education Level _____

College / University _____

Business Name _____

Field of Business _____

Website _____

Product or Service Provided _____

_____

Personal Strengthens _____

_____

Personal Weaknesses _____

_____

Coach or Advisor _____

Name _____

Hometown _____

Date of Birth _____

Highest Education Level _____

College / University _____

Business Name _____

Field of Business _____

Website _____

Product or Service Provided _____

_____

Personal Strengthens _____

_____

Personal Weaknesses _____

_____

Coach or Advisor _____

Name _____

Hometown _____

Date of Birth _____

Highest Education Level _____

College / University _____

Business Name _____

Field of Business _____

Website _____

Product or Service Provided _____

_____

Personal Strengthens _____

_____

Personal Weaknesses _____

_____

Coach or Advisor _____

Name _____

Hometown _____

Date of Birth _____

Highest Education Level _____

College / University _____

Business Name _____

Field of Business _____

Website _____

Product or Service Provided _____

_____

Personal Strengthens _____

_____

Personal Weaknesses _____

_____

Coach or Advisor _____

Name _____

Hometown _____

Date of Birth _____

Highest Education Level _____

College / University _____

Business Name _____

Field of Business _____

Website _____

Product or Service Provided _____

_____

Personal Strengthens _____

_____

Personal Weaknesses _____

_____

Coach or Advisor _____

Name _____

Hometown _____

Date of Birth _____

Highest Education Level _____

College / University _____

Business Name _____

Field of Business _____

Website _____

Product or Service Provided _____

_____

Personal Strengthens _____

_____

Personal Weaknesses _____

_____

Coach or Advisor _____

Name _____

Hometown _____

Date of Birth _____

Highest Education Level _____

College / University _____

Business Name _____

Field of Business _____

Website _____

Product or Service Provided _____

_____

Personal Strengthens _____

_____

Personal Weaknesses _____

_____

Coach or Advisor _____

Name _____

Hometown _____

Date of Birth _____

Highest Education Level _____

College / University _____

Business Name _____

Field of Business _____

Website _____

Product or Service Provided _____

_____

Personal Strengthens _____

_____

Personal Weaknesses _____

_____

Coach or Advisor _____

Name _____

Hometown _____

Date of Birth _____

Highest Education Level _____

College / University _____

Business Name _____

Field of Business _____

Website _____

Product or Service Provided _____

_____

Personal Strengthens _____

_____

Personal Weaknesses _____

_____

Coach or Advisor _____

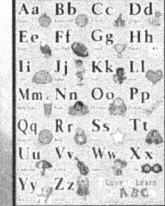

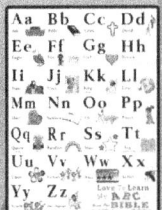

DEXTER J. HUMPHREY

Dexter J. Humphrey
Educator, Engineer,
Entrepreneur & Author
B.S.E.E, M.A.I.S., M.I.E.E

A former electrical engineer, Dexter Humphrey is the founder of Jasa Leadership Group LLC, an educational resource firm providing products, strategies and initiatives for students & academic leaders. Mr. Humphrey is an education and business consultant with expertise in entrepreneurship, collegiate success strategies, literacy initiatives, and academic aptitude enhancements.

Read more from Dexter at www.JasaLeadership.com

DEXTER THE EDUCATOR™

WWW.DEXTERHUMPHREY.COM

www.ingramcontent.com/pod-product-compliance
Lightning Source LLC
Chambersburg PA
CBHW052336220526
45472CB00001B/455